The Retirement Planning Book

The easy-to-understand, must-read
book if you want to retire comfortably

By Douglas Goldstein, CFP®

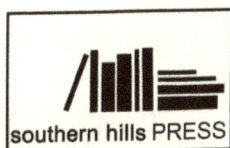

southern hills PRESS

First published 2013

Published by Southern Hills Press, Pittsburgh, PA, USA

Book ISBN: 978-1-933882-14-7

1. Retirement planning   2. Financial planning   3. Investment basics

For further information, email: info@profile-financial.com

CONTENT

INTRODUCTION

Everyone talks about retirement, but are you doing anything to prepare for it? According to the U.S. Department of Labor, less than half of the workforce has calculated how much they need to save in order to retire.

People often look to their retirement as free time. But there is no such thing as "free" time – retirement has its own bills to pay. How do you meet your expenses when pension plans only cover a small percentage of your living costs?

That's where personal savings come into play.

How can you save and plan for something so far in the future?

How much money will you actually need for retirement?

When should you start saving, and exactly what do you need to do?

Retirement planning is a difficult task, but not impossible.

The secret to retirement planning is that it takes work, determination, and commitment to achieving a goal.

There is one more thing that can help you in your journey toward retirement – *The Retirement Planning Book.*

The journey from envisioning your retirement lifestyle to planning a budget, and from establishing your investment portfolio to enjoying the fruits of your labor should not be taken alone.

The information in *The Retirement Planning Book* will guide you through the stages of your financial life, leading up to the day when you retire... and then some.

Though this book covers a great deal of critical information, make sure to work with a qualified financial planner to guide you along the way. Financial planners have the education and experience to help you through every stage of planning your retirement. Read this book to help you create a fabulous retirement.

Thanks for taking the time to read this book. If you have any questions or ideas, please be in touch.

Douglas Goldstein, CFP®
doug@profile-financial.com

SECTION ONE:

PREPARING FOR RETIREMENT

Retirement Planning Isn't Only About Numbers

Retirement planning is not only financial.

Retirement planning is more than analyzing your expenses and investment accounts. It is a deeply personal journey of who you are, what you like to do, and what type of legacy you wish to create. Retirement planning has a financial component, but before you gather all your bank statements, first collect your thoughts.

What will you do after you retire?

You can only begin to determine the financial considerations and how much money you will need to fund the lifestyle you want once you have answered the question above.

A good starting point for retirement planning is looking at your parents and grandparents. How long did they live? While your genetic propensity to longevity is beyond your control, life expectancy calculators may be useful in projecting how long your money needs to last. As lifespans increase, savings accounts need to be stretched further.

While an "end date" to your retirement plan may seem disconcerting, consider adding several years to actuarial projections to make sure you don't outlive your money. Indeed, Prudential's recent ad campaign asserts that people with life expectancies of 150 years have already been born. Living long not only means many birthdays surrounded with family and friends, but also means more chances for unexpected expenses and unanticipated events that can potentially derail even the most carefully made plan.

As you prepare for retirement, flexibility, discipline, and financial calculators remain your best tools.

Retirement remains an elusive dream for many workers. However, proper planning can help bring the dream into reality. Economic insecurity and worker confidence levels aside, the fact is that many retirees find themselves retired earlier than anticipated. Either poor health or work conditions beyond their control impose a retirement date.

While you can't control the unexpected, you can control your response. Proper retirement planning can pave the path to make the next stage of life as rewarding as possible, making sure you have the funds to do what you want to do.

What Type of Lifestyle Do You Want in Retirement?

Many aspects of retirement planning are based upon actuarial charts and life expectancy calculators that tell you how long the average person lives. It's difficult to plan for a phase of your life based on an assumption that may or may not actualize. Even if the statistics were correct, they don't take into account the chances of something unforeseen happening that may alter original projections. However, since we don't have crystal balls to predict the future, financial planners base projections on receiving statistics and facts that are as accurate as possible. Retirement planning assumes a degree of uncertainty.

Three factors to take into consideration when planning your retirement lifestyle are:

Be realistic in your choice of lifestyle

While it is true that retirement brings more free time, take an objective look at yourself before sitting down to write your list of the things you want to accomplish. Health, finances, family obligations, and other possible constraints on your lifestyle should be taken into consideration. Being realistic about what you want to accomplish will help you avoid the frustration associated with planning a lifestyle that is impossible to achieve.

The sad truth about expenses

Too many people plan their retirement lifestyle budgets depending upon decreases in expenses. It might be true that downsizing from a big, family-friendly house to smaller, less expensive, living accommodations will save money, but what about other living expenses? The home repairs you were able to do on your own might require a contractor as your ability to do certain tasks becomes limited by the aging process.

Even if you are in good health as you approach or enter retirement, a serious illness could significantly add to your expenses. Factor into your budget the flexibility to meet unknown expenses.

Get professional advice

Financial planners know the perils that come from unrealistic or ill-planned lifestyles. Discuss your lifestyle choices with your financial planner to make certain that your budget and retirement fund are up to the task of meeting your needs. A certified financial planner can't magically make money appear where there wasn't enough before, but he can help you manage your expectations.

How Much Money Do You Need to Save?

Traditionally, the rule of thumb in retirement planning is that you need 70-80% of your current income during retirement. This lower figure represents all the expenses (transportation, income tax, etc.) that may not appear in your retirement budget. However, basing the size of your retirement nest egg on the size of your income target doesn't always make sense.

It's like basing your grocery shopping on the size of your refrigerator. You don't shop just to fill up the fridge. What really matters is the type of food you like to eat and how large your appetite is, not the size of the storage container.

Similarly, your current income levels are less relevant to retirement planning than your spending patterns. Your spending, not your income, reflects your lifestyle. And you have to save enough to allow for the retirement lifestyle you want.

There is no magic number of "how much" you need saved before you retire.

"How much" you need to retire is a personal decision – it depends on what you want to do, your lifestyle, your current savings and projected income, your risk level, what type of inheritance you want to leave behind, etc.

While it may make sense to save as much as possible, you need to balance your future needs with your current expenses. If you already have "enough" saved and are confident that your pensions will be sizeable, maybe you can spend more now. Balancing future needs against current expenses is difficult. However, having a financial plan that looks at your overall cash-flow, both pre-and post-retirement, can provide a realistic number of how much you should save now.

While it's prudent to prepare for tomorrow, don't forget about today and make sure your savings plan meets both your current and future needs.

Where to Begin: Planning Your Retirement

The first step of your retirement plan is creating your own retirement wish list without any concerns about cost. Determining if you can afford the lifestyle on your wish list comes later. Until you know what you want, you cannot plan your budget or the savings schedule needed to meet it.

Plan your retirement savings

Calculating how much you need to save to afford your dream retirement depends on your current age, your anticipated retirement age, your current nest egg, your anticipated pensions, how much you can save between now and then, and your risk tolerance in investing. It is important to remember that all of these factors are interrelated – if you have great pension plans which you feel confident won't default, or a sizeable current portfolio, you may be a ble to enjoy a nice lifestyle with less in savings. But if your current savings and anticipated pension plan payments are both small, you may need to save more now...or postpone retirement. A professional retirement (financial) planner can assist you in doing the calculations to arrive at the amount you must set aside on a regular basis to fund your retirement dreams.

What do you want and what can you afford?

Make sure your plan is written and refer back to it regularly. Update your plan based on both changes in your desires and changes in market returns. If you made a retirement plan while in your 50s, and you are now in your 60s, your definition of the ideal retirement lifestyle might have changed. And your retirement plan and investment structure might need to change accordingly.

WHEN SHOULD I RETIRE?

Today, most businesses don't have a compulsory retirement age, and 67 is an average rather than a specific time to hang up your hat. Medical advances, increased lifespans, and lifestyle changes make determining the perfect retirement age a highly individual decision.

Sooner or later?

Most countries have a lower age when you can begin to get a State pension, but will reward you with larger payments if you wait until you are older before claiming payments. For example, Americans can start getting Social Security at age 62, but will get a monthly payment that is about 30% less than they would have gotten if they waited until full retirement age (67). And, if they wait until age 70, they will get an extra 8% for every year's delay after full retirement age. Don't wait beyond that, though, since the increase stops at age 70. Therefore, the question is whether you take a pension from the minimum age of retirement, or whether you wait until you're older, when you'll receive more money. You need to balance your more immediate needs (do you have other streams of income) against larger payments later on.

Is it really for you?

On paper, like so many other things, pushing off your pension may sound like a great idea. But is it really appropriate for you?

While there are some energetic seniors in the working world, others start to feel the physical strain of working every day, especially if this is what they've been doing for the past several decades. Others would rather use their remaining energy to spend time with their grandchildren or to realize their dreams.

Do you have the means?

Before making a decision, look at your resources. Can you live entirely off your savings if you decide to retire before you are fully eligible for government and work-related pensions? Or do you need to work a few extra years in order to receive higher pension benefits?

Empty traps

Sometimes a bird in the hand is worth more than many empty traps. If you begin claiming pension payments at an earlier age (albeit a lesser payment), you are actually receiving *something*, rather than waiting and having your pension company possibly default on pension payments, or missing out if you don't live as long as expected.

Your financial advisor can help you calculate the total anticipated pension payment to be received in either scenario. While knowing the anticipated sums in multiple scenarios can help make a decision as to when you should retire, don't let the number be your only deciding factor, since many variables (i.e., living significantly longer or shorter than actuarial table predictions) can skew the calculation. Make the decision as to when to retire after jointly considering *both* financial and emotional factors.

The Costs and Benefits of Early Retirement

Early retirement may sound appealing. But like most things, timing and planning are essential.

Assuming that you have planned your retirement with the help of a professional financial advisor, you should know how much money you will need to support your future lifestyle.

If your retirement income won't suffice, you may need to consider part-time work. Or, you may simply want to keep a toehold in the working world. If you plan to work and collect a state pension, check how much you can earn without jeopardizing both your current and future benefits.

Retirement accounts

Many employer-funded pension plans specify an age when an employee is entitled to retire with benefits. Retiring earlier than your plan allows could mean having to fund your early retirement with another source of funds. Retirement accounts such as IRA and 401(k) plans are not usually available until you reach age 59 and a half. Israeli work-related plans also have a minimum age for distribution, and the projections on your annual statements are often made with later retirement figures. Taking the money earlier could mean paying substantial penalties and/or receiving lower payouts.

Don't give up on early retirement

Just because the financial weight of stopping to work may discourage you, don't give up on a dream completely. Many people switch careers later in life, and as they do it, they take a mini-retirement. Even though stepping out of the workforce for a few months costs money, it can also give you a new view on a life, a well-deserved break, and the chance to see what retirement feels like. Maybe after sitting at home for a few months you will begin to miss the daily work routine. On the other hand, you may enjoy it so much that you will be willing to live a lower-cost lifestyle in exchange for not having to work. The theoretical vs. actual worlds of personal finance are, in fact, quite different. Take the time to figure out what works for you.

THREE RULES FOR EARLY RETIREMENT SUCCESS

According to a recent Gallup survey, the average retirement age in the United States is 67. This is up from a decade ago, when 63 years of age was the norm. In Israel, the standard retirement age for men is 67 and 62 for women.

Although retirement ages are rising, many people still choose to retire early. If this is something you want to do, take the following three rules into account before making your decision:

Know the risks and be prepared for them

If you think you have enough money saved to retire before the standard retirement age, ask yourself if your plans are realistic. If your investments fail to outpace inflation, do you have a contingency plan? Can you afford to live on your savings and investment income until you are eligible for governmental pensions and can receive your work pension benefits? Answering the "what if" questions could spell the difference between a successful early retirement and financial disaster.

Control spending

If retirement was a foot race, it would be a marathon instead of a sprint. Unfortunately, too many early retirees are sprinters when it comes to spending. Younger retirees tend to be active individuals who are prone to spending on hobbies, travel, and entertainment, without thinking ahead.

Free time is rarely, if ever, truly free. Increased leisure time usually means increased spending. You might not be able to control the economy, but you can control your spending.

When you were working, there was the opportunity to increase income with additional hours or changing jobs. Unless you consider part-time retirement work, retirement depletes your savings, as opposed to increasing them. Therefore, you need to live within your budget and control spending. Ideally, your budget has a line for a "slush" fund that allows for discretionary spending, but expenditures need to be kept in check.

Be flexible

Stay flexible to be able to adapt to life changes. If medical expenses increase, you'll need to decrease other expenses. If the market doesn't follow your predictions, you might have to withdraw less from your accounts.

Sometimes retirees think that if they run out of money they can get a job. While flexible thinking is a marker of a successful retirement, re-entering the work force may not be an option. Perhaps your health won't allow it, or you will face age-discrimination from employers who want to hire younger (and cheaper) employees.

If you choose early retirement as an option, be aware that you are also choosing to address certain risks and are prepared to lower your spending in case you need to stretch your resources further.

Is it Too Late to Begin Planning?

Ideally, you should have begun planning your retirement when you received your very first paycheck. But if you are like most people, that didn't happen.

Whether you just woke up to the fact that retirement is around the corner, or if it is still decades away, there is plenty you can do to prepare for the next stage of life.

Savings + growth = retirement

After you completed your retirement wish list, calculate what your anticipated retirement lifestyle will cost. Then, re-evaluate your goals to determine what is reasonable. There is a certain amount of give and take in creating the budget and you may have to negotiate with yourself/your spouse to decide whether you wish to work X years longer in order to be able to afford your vacation home, or if it is worthwhile to you to downsize your house in order to be able to afford earlier retirement. There is no right and wrong answer… except when it comes to taking on more risk than you can afford.

Big numbers

If you haven't put together a written financial plan yet, you may not realize that the amount needed to sustain your current lifestyle could be in the millions of dollars. People spending $50,000 to $100,000 a year could easily need $1.5 million to $3 million in liquid assets to assure that they will have enough cash flow to support themselves for the rest of their lives.

Before you give up any hope of retiring, no one is suggesting that the millions need to come only from your monthly salary. There is a simple truth about savings: money properly invested can grow in time to meet your goals. Compound interest, time, and patience are important tools in helping your money grow.

Make lifestyle changes now to help you later

One way to fund savings is to decrease your expenses. Live below your means. Take a cold, hard look at your spending habits and decide which expenses to eliminate. Always pay yourself (make deposits into your savings and investment accounts) before you pay other bills.

It's never too late to start

Starting a retirement savings plan is not impossible. All you need is a little planning, the discipline to find the money, and the commitment to succeed.

How to Save

Saving money is easier said than done. Once you decide to save, what should you do with the money you are no longer spending?

First, pay off debt. Lower your expenses to live below your means. Once your debt is paid off, continue depositing monthly payments into your own savings account.

Set goals. Even small amounts make a difference. As long as you are saving something, you are moving in the right direction. Don't be fooled into thinking an amount is too small to make a difference. At the very least, it will solidify in your mind that you are a saver, actively working on a retirement plan.

What should you do with your savings?

The first part of your savings plan should be your emergency fund, invested directly in the bank. This way, you'll have easy access to it if and when you should need it.

Then, consider placing funds in investment vehicles like:

Stocks – are shares of a company. In purchasing a stock, you buy an actual portion of the company and can participate in its long-term growth. Stock owners earn money from the long-term appreciation of the company (eventually selling shares at a higher price than what they paid for them), and by receiving periodic dividends (distribution of the company's profit). Stocks are considered risky investments, since there is the real potential of significant loss of principal.

Bonds – are loans you make to a company or other entity. Bondholders earn money from the interest payments the company/government/municipality pays for the privilege of borrowing cash. Since bondholders generally know the interest payment schedule in advance, bonds are useful investments for folks who want to receive regular income from their investment account (as opposed to growth). While generally considered more conservative than stocks, depending on the company and type of bond, there is a chance of losing principal with bonds too.

Mutual funds – are baskets of different investments, as opposed to individual stocks or bonds, and are used to diversify an account and by spreading out exposure. There are many different types of mutual funds, each carrying its own risk level and pros and cons. Spend time researching the fund before you buy. Don't just focus on the past performance of the investment. Rather, look at the management, the investment style, the asset allocation, the fees, the risks, and the volatility. Though many people pick funds themselves, others get counsel from licensed advisors. For long-term savings, mutual funds that invest in stocks often make more sense than buying individual stocks since the funds offer both instant diversification and professional management. Always read the marketing documents and prospectus before investing money.

Liquid investments – at the same time that you want to invest your savings in one or more of the different investment vehicles mentioned above, it is important to keep a portion of your investments liquid. Short-term CDs, money market funds, and cold cash are all considered liquid investments.

All the investments described here have risks; discuss them with your advisor before purchasing. Investment advisors frequently use several of these investment vehicles in combination in order to set up a well-balanced portfolio that maximizes returns and minimizes the potential for loss. Once you have made the decision to save, do it efficiently so that your money works its hardest for you.

DO YOU NEED AN EMERGENCY FUND?

Financial advisors suggest maintaining an emergency savings fund ranging from three to six months of non-discretionary expenses. Having a set amount set aside for emergencies protects your retirement savings, and helps you avoid going into serious debt when a fiscal crisis occurs. While it may be emotionally difficult to keep money in a liquid (read: not high-yielding account), having the money easily accessible in case of need is crucial.

Can't retirement savings be considered an emergency fund?

Some believe that an emergency fund is a waste of time and money, as they figure they could always access their retirement funds in an emergency. However, there are two reasons that make tapping into retirement funds for emergencies a bad idea.

First, there are often tax penalties for withdrawing money from retirement funds. The tax-free incentives are meant to encourage savings, so the government discourages withdrawing from these accounts by charging stiff penalties to the tune of 10% plus tax. You may also be tempted to borrow against your retirement plan, but depending on the terms of the program, the cost of borrowing against your retirement funds can be quite high. Anyway, do you really want to put money into an account and then pay interest for the privilege of borrowing back your own money?

Second, if you withdraw money from retirement funds for emergencies, will you really repay it? Most people repay money they owe to someone else quicker than repaying themselves. Over time, not repaying withdrawals can have a serious impact on the size of your retirement fund.

Pre- or post-retirement

Creating an emergency fund protects your retirement savings. Make sure the emergency fund is liquid, so you can use it if necessary. The emergency fund protects you both pre- and post-retirement. By having money readily available, you won't need to withdraw your principal, upon which your future income may rely.

What constitutes an emergency?

Use your emergency fund wisely. Buying a new couch is not an emergency. Paying bills in case of disability or unemployment is. Some areas, like a financing a new washing machine or major auto repairs fall into a gray area. Consider creating an un-emergency fund for periodic, expected expenses like these.

Your Emergency Fund: An Investment or an Insurance Policy?

Putting aside money for an emergency is a good idea, but for an emergency fund to be fully accessible, it needs to be in a liquid asset. Liquid assets, like money markets and CDs receive low interest. So why is putting money aside that won't grow a good investment?

Reasons not to invest your emergency fund

The money you put aside for emergencies should be enough to cover several months of fixed income. The size of your emergency fund should reflect your risk comfort level. Financial advisors use three to six months of essential living expenses as the benchmark, and sometimes as much as twelve months, depending on the client.

Moving your emergency fund money into investment vehicles that yield a higher return involves greater risk, and you can't afford to take a risk with this money, because it has to be there in full, if and when needed.

Your emergency fund needs to be liquid, so it can be accessed instantly, without penalties. If it is invested in a risky investment, then its real value might drop. If it is in an illiquid investment, you may not be able to sell it when faced with a bill. You want your emergency fund to be there if the time comes when you need it. Remember, emergencies don't wait for a bull market.

Review your personal life and work situation. Someone who works in an unstable industry such as construction, where layoffs are common, or on a commission-based salary, may need a larger emergency fund. Likewise, a single person may face fewer emergencies than a family with many children, and his fund may not need to be as large.

If you find yourself jumping from one emergency to another, keeping your emergency fund topped up in a safe, easily accessible investment vehicle is an important insurance policy against having to withdraw from your retirement fund or sell out other investments.

THE ANTI-EMERGENCY FUND

No matter how well you plan, unexpected surprises can derail your budget. While it's a good idea to have an emergency fund, if you have one, how do you decide when to dip into the fund? Is replacing a broken microwave an emergency?

There are a set amount of expenses that aren't emergencies, but they regularly occur – replacing car tires, a child's lost knapsack, etc. Even a relatively minor expense can derail a sensitive budget. An anti-emergency fund helps save for variable expenses (both expected and unexpected) that inevitably take place. Insurance premiums, birthdays, and higher heating costs in the winter all fall into the category of inevitable expenses.

Planning for the "it's bound to happen" events can help eliminate financial stress. In all the years I've helped clients create retirement plans, only one client wanted to include a line in his budget for the eventual replacement of large appliances. How will you pay for new appliances if you don't have extra disposable income? If you're forced to dip into pension savings to afford a new refrigerator, you may be faced with penalties, taxes, and the inevitable decline in your account's value.

Planning and saving can help prevent the fastballs in everyday life from turning into a crisis. My in-laws have a jar by the washing machine, and every time they do a load, they pay a dollar, earmarked for the inevitable cost of a new machine/repair. Your "anti-emergency fund" can either be a separate account, or a line item in your budget. If you budget for repairs and then don't need them, then the additional cash can cushion your account.

The markets aren't the only force that can wreak havoc on your savings. Having both an emergency fund and an anti-emergency fund can prevent a surprise from turning into a fiscal catastrophe. Fully funded emergency and anti-emergency accounts can safeguard your retirement savings and provide cash when you need it most.

How an Automatic Savings Plan Gets You into the Savings Swing

Automatic savings plans make it easy to get into and keep the savings habit. They work especially well for building an emergency fund, and can also be used to make sure you meet your regular long-term savings goals.

Automatic transfer basics

Most banks offer an automatic transfer plan, which transfers a fixed amount from your checking account into a savings account on a recurring basis that you designate. Once you choose the amount, the date of the first transfer, and the frequency at which subsequent transfers will take place, your savings plan becomes a reality and isn't put on hold when something unexpected or 'more important' comes up.

The benefit of this automatic savings plan is that your account builds up without any effort or thought on your part other than the initial setup. If the transfers happen automatically, you won't forget to make them, and the money is saved before it can be diverted for other uses. Out of sight, out of mind.

Resist temptation

Refrain from referring to your emergency fund as your savings account. Training yourself to look at the money you are putting aside as being only for emergencies will help you resist the temptation to use the funds for other expenditures. If you find yourself making withdrawals from the emergency fund to pay monthly expenses, then you need to reevaluate your budget and savings plan.

Don't be afraid to admit that the amount you designated for savings each month might have been unrealistic, or that you might have underestimated your expenses. Savings plans are always works in progress requiring periodic review and adjusting.

Three types of automatic transfer

Ideally every month your accounts will see three automatic transfers:

- To work-related pension funds,

- To personal savings accounts,

- To your emergency fund.

If the money is automatically withdrawn from your account you won't feel the "pain" of having less money to spend, and you will be assured the most important payments, to yourself and your future, are actually being made on a regular basis.

A Written Financial Plan for Retirement

A builder recently expressed his concerns about not being financially prepared for retirement. He had been putting money aside now and then, but it was not enough to provide him with the retirement lifestyle he envisioned. When I asked him about his retirement plan, he answered, "Retirement plan? I just put aside whatever I can afford each month. Some months, there might be more than others."

This fellow would cringe at the thought of building a house without a proper set of blueprints. Imagine how clients would feel if a builder told them that the construction schedule was a little work today and maybe a little more next week, but if something else came along, then nothing would get done. They would look for a new, more reliable builder, with set plans to finish the project.

The purpose of a written financial plan

A written financial (retirement) plan is like the construction plans for a new home. It tells you what you need in order to build enough wealth to support you during retirement. It starts with a vision of your retirement lifestyle (your final house) and helps you put that vision into action by establishing financial goals and showing you how to meet them in a particular timeline.

Defining what you must do

Saving money is nice, but your financial plan defines what your required monthly savings target is. Once you know how much you need to make it to the end of the plan, you can work backwards, taking stock of your current savings and anticipated cash-flow. With that data, create a savings plan based on your risk tolerance and expectations of market returns. While past performance is not a guarantee of future results, financial planners often use a statistical model called a Monte Carlo Simulation. This type of analysis tests your particular financial situation in thousands of possible market scenarios. You can adjust the variables, like savings amounts and asset allocation, to suit your needs and goals and test possible outcomes.

Getting the most from your investments

A financial plan not only tells you how much you need to put aside on an annual basis, but it helps to calculate a diversified asset allocation that will best meet your goals. Studies have shown that a proper asset allocation that changes to meet your investment needs is one of the best determinants of successful investing, much more so than "timing the market."

A comprehensive financial plan includes a review of health insurance, pension plans, stock options, and personal savings and spending patterns.

How to Create a Financial Plan

A written financial plan is an indispensable tool for retirement planning. But how do you create one?

Even if you are a "DIY- Do It Yourself" person, consider going to a Certified Financial Planner™ professional for advice. CFPs have years of training, continuing education requirements, and expertise at looking at the overall financial picture. Furthermore, you benefit from their experience, which can help you save time and avoid costly mistakes.

Even more important, a professional financial advisor has an objective, unemotional insight into your future goals and aspirations. Creating the plan and setting up the investments are two separate steps. A professional advisor can do both, or just help you create the plan.

Look at the big picture

A professional financial advisor looks at all aspects of a person's finances, including budgeting, investing, retirement, insurance, estate planning, and saving for long- and short-term goals. Financial planners develop a strategy to enable these separate components of your financial life to work together in harmony. Are your investments positioned both to protect the principal and grow/provide income, or are you just focused on growth? Focusing on just one aspect, like growth, may expose you to too much risk.

Setting up a budget and savings plan might seem like an easy task, but people frequently focus only on a single goal without considering how the many aspects of their financial life fit together. For instance, in order to achieve optimal diversification, it may not be prudent to own many stocks in the same business sector as you work in. If you and your spouse work in the same startup and have stock options, your salaries and future growth of your portfolio are all based on the same company. If it were to go bankrupt, chances are your retirement plans would go down the drain too.

Financial planning isn't just for the wealthy

While wealthy folks frequently employ a financial planner to help them diversify their already sizeable portfolio, it is important to stress that financial planning isn't just for the affluent. Perhaps "regular" folks need it more in order to optimize their limited resources and maximize their chances of succeeding financially.

A financial advisor helps to get you from the vague, "I want to plan for retirement," to formulating a detailed vision of your retirement lifestyle. Using a budget showing projected discretionary and non-discretionary expenses, your advisor analyzes the sources of income that will be available to you in retirement and helps you develop a savings and investment strategy to achieve your retirement lifestyle.

Financial planning does not begin and end with retirement. It is comprehensive and addresses pre-retirement, post-retirement, and the legacy you wish to leave behind.

Retirement Savings Tips for the Older Worker

If you are approaching retirement and realize that your retirement plan never made the leap from planning to execution, don't despair. There are a few things you can do to build your retirement fund.

Take stock of your retirement benefits

Contact *Bituach Leumi* and/or Social Security to find out how much your government pension payments will be. You can obtain this information online, by calling the National Phone Center on *6050, or at your local office. (To find your local office, go to www.btl.gov.il)

Contact your company's human resources office or insurance agent to find out your anticipated work pension benefits. Be aware that you may not be given a specific number since benefits may be dependent on the actual return on the investments in your particular plans.

Maximize your contributions

In the United States, many employers have 401(k) and 403(b) voluntary contribution plans, but fewer than half of the people who have such plans available to them actually sign up and participate in them. Now is the time to maximize any contributions you can make. Even if you would rather see the extra salary appear in your monthly paycheck, try to remain forward thinking in contributing the maximum to your retirement plans.

Older workers are often allowed to make a "catch up contribution" to their U.S. retirement plans. Check with your accountant to see if you can take advantage of the extra tax-free savings. Even if you participate in a 401(k) or other plan through your job, you can also contribute to a Roth IRA.

Pay off debt

Look at your overall debt, including credit card balances, mortgages, and personal loans. Not only does debt limit the amount of money you have available to put away for retirement, but it also increases your expenses if you take any of the debt into retirement with you. Would you rather pay interest payments or buy something you want/need?

Commit to paying off as much debt as you can, as quickly as possible. This is particularly true of high-interest-rate credit card debt. Pay off the balances and pledge to avoid incurring future balances. If you can't control spending on credit cards, consider moving to an all-cash model.

Arriving at the retirement planning table late is better than not at all. Although planning and saving are more challenging the closer you are to retirement, as long as latecomers are armed with determination and discipline, they should be able to improve their situation.

SECTION TWO:

INVESTING FOR RETIREMENT

EMPLOYER-SPONSORED
RETIREMENT PLANS

While many people consider governmental Social Security payments to be their pension, the current economic situation puts a question mark on how long America will be able to continue with substantial payments. Countries world-wide are considering revamping their payout structure. Indeed, Israeli *Bituach Leumi* payments are lower than the minimum wage. Therefore, personal savings and work-related pension plans gain importance in providing for a secure retirement.

Employer-sponsored retirement plans offer workers an easy, readily accessible vehicle through which they can prepare for retirement. Frequently, payments into retirement plans are made from pre-tax dollars, and employee payments may be matched by the employer. Since saving this way increases the leverage of any deposit you make, it is prudent to make the maximum deposits in any work-related savings plan.

However, not all retirement plans are the same. How a plan is funded and the benefits employees can expect to receive when they retire may differ from one plan to another. Defined benefit retirement plans and defined contribution retirement plans are the two most commonly found employer-sponsored plans.

Defined benefit retirement plans

Defined benefit retirement plans offer employees a specified benefit each month when they retire. Funded by the employer, the monthly benefit is usually stated as a fixed dollar amount, or it might be based upon factors such as the number of years that you worked for the company, your earnings, and your age. Some defined benefit plans use a percentage of your earnings for your last three to five years prior to retirement to calculate the benefit amount. However, these days, fewer and fewer companies offer defined benefit plans because of the uncertainty of the market. They don't want to be responsible for paying a pre-determined amount to their retired workers in case the market doesn't perform as expected. Instead, many workplaces offer defined contribution plans.

Defined contribution retirement plans

A defined contribution retirement plan doesn't offer a specific benefit amount at retirement. Under this type of plan, you, your employer, or both contribute to your retirement account. The money contributed from your pretax dollars is invested on your behalf. The size of the fund when you retire will depend upon the amount that is contributed and the investment performance through the years. An example of a defined contribution plans is a 401(k). When you stop working for a company, you can normally roll over the 401(k) into an IRA (individual retirement account), which allows you greater control of the money and still maintains its tax beneficial status.

Contact your employer's plan administrator or human resources office for details about how your company's retirement plan operates. Every year, check your paperwork to make sure that all contributions were accurately recorded.

Israeli Pension Plans

Israeli law requires that full-time workers who have worked for longer than six months receive a pension plan through their employers. This is part of the government's plan of making sure individuals have private pensions to supplement their governmental pensions. Pensions are a highly regulated field, and as such the details are in constant flux. Check with your pension administrator or insurance agent for the updated specifics related to your individual plan.

Work Pensions

The Israeli government requires employers to offer a pension plan that provides a monthly benefit. Both employer and worker make contributions into the plan, and the employee's contributions are paid from pre-tax shekels, providing a substantial tax benefit.

Standard pension plans are often split into several parts: savings (towards the eventual pension payments), life and disability insurance, and severance pay.

Within certain limitations, the employee may elect how the premiums are apportioned, and choose among different asset allocation models. Not every pension plan has every option, so be sure that you understand all the details of your specific plan.

Typical plans include:

Bituach minahalim – contains savings, insurance (both life and disability), and severance pay,

Kupat gemel – tax-free savings plan without the insurance element,

Keren pensia – similar to a *bituach minahalim* plan, but the savings component here is in a joint fund (as opposed to being managed individually).

Customize your pension plan to your needs

The contents of your work-related pension plans should fit into your asset allocation model. If you own life insurance directly with an insurance company, you may prefer to focus your *bituach minahalim* on savings (especially with their tax-deferred advantage) and minimize the insurance dimension (which may cost more in the plan than if bought separately).

Keren Hishtalmut

Some employers also offer a tax-beneficial savings plan called *Keren hishtalmut*, which uses money set aside by both the employer and the employee. These funds are closed for six years, and there is a tax penalty if withdrawn during this period. Though originally intended to be used for continuing education purposes, often people use it for other recreational purposes. However, the wisest course may be to use it for retirement.

The investment structure within a plan is chosen by the employee. The insurance companies are governed by regulations on how they can invest the funds, but it's up to the employee to choose the specific investment allocation model. Make sure you periodically re-evaluate how your funds are allocated, since what could have been an appropriate fund when you began investing may no longer be the best choice for closer to retirement.

How IRAs Fit Into Your Retirement Plans

An IRA is an individual retirement account into which you put money for your retirement. It offers you the opportunity to squirrel away pretax dollars for the future. An IRA is not an investment, but merely a vehicle into which you deposit your money and in which you can buy stocks, mutual funds, bonds, and other assets. If you live and work in Israel, you may not be able to contribute to an IRA. In fact, accountants in Israel debate about IRA accounts' tax-deferred status in Israel for those people who moved to Israel and have IRAs in America.

In any case, it helps to understand their structures. There are several different types of IRAs:

Traditional IRAs

In a traditional IRA, you receive a U.S. tax deduction for the amount contributed to your IRA up to a yearly maximum of $5,500 for the 2013 tax year. The annual contribution limit is $6,500 if you are 50 years of age or older.

The money in the account remains tax-deferred until you withdraw it. This includes the dividends, capital gains, and interest on the funds you contributed to the account. Therefore, it may be prudent to purchase growth investments (as opposed to money markets or CDs) to maximize the tax-free growth. But be aware that if the investments lose value, you cannot write that loss off on your tax returns.

Distributions taken after age 59 ½ are taxed as ordinary income. Distributions taken earlier are liable for a 10% tax penalty, as well as tax on the withdrawn sum. Once you turn 70, you are subject to mandatory distributions.

Roth IRAs

Roth IRAs have similar contribution limits as traditional IRAs, but you cannot deduct the amount of the contribution on your income tax return. The Roth IRA may be a better choice for some people because the distributions taken after the age of 59 ½ are tax-free. There are no mandatory distributions, so if you wish you can leave the money in the account for your estate to distribute.

Talk to your financial advisor because there are income and filing rules that apply to Roth IRAs. Use a free online calculator comparing Roth and traditional IRAs to help you to decide which works best for you.

SEP IRAs and Simple IRAs

Simplified Employee Pension IRAs (SEP) and simple IRAs are usually associated with self-employed individuals or small businesses with only a few employees. They allow an employer to make contributions with higher annual limits for the employees and owners. SEP IRAs are simpler than a pension plan, but more complex than Roth or traditional IRAs. Consult with your financial advisor before setting these up.

Where you invest your retirement money is important, but the account that you use to make the investment is equally important. Oftentimes people prefer to buy stocks in their taxable accounts because capital gains tax rates are lower than the tax on interest. Then, they choose to purchase taxable bonds might in their retirement accounts because of the tax advantages the account offers. However, these are not fixed rules, and each case should be examined individually.

What You Should Know about 401(k) Retirement Plans

In America, it's common for employers to offer their workers the opportunity to participate in defined contribution plans, where they have greater control of how their money is invested. The most common defined benefit pension plan is a 401(k).

What is a 401(k)?

A 401(k) plan is a plan where an employee chooses to have a portion of his pretax wages contributed to a qualified plan. The definition of "a qualified plan" is that it meets Internal Revenue Code standards to be considered for tax-favored status. The plan gets its name from section 401(k) of the IRC that is applicable to it.

The money contributed to the plan is invested in any number of investment vehicles, including stocks, bonds, or mutual funds. Capital gains, interest, or dividends realized on the investment of the contributions are not taxed. This has the double advantage that both contributions and growth are tax-free.

Benefits of a 401(k) retirement plan

401(k) plans have two main benefits: tax-free status and matching contributions between employer and worker.

Pretax contributions that are excluded from income, and the fact that no taxes are paid on the return on the investment of the money until its disbursement, make taxes a leading reason for using a 401(k) for retirement planning.

Many employers offer 401(k) plans where they match all or a percentage of the contributions made by their employees. This is an ideal way to make your retirement fund grow even faster. Look upon it as a gift from your employer, but the gift comes with a string attached. The contributions you make to a 401(k) are vested immediately. This means that if you leave your place of employment, the money you invested is yours to take with you. This is not the case with the money contributed by your employer. Those funds might not vest until you have worked there for a specified number of years. If you are planning to change jobs, check with your employer's plan administrator to find out what your vested rights are before making a decision that could leave a substantial amount of money behind.

Using your 401(k) in an emergency

You might be able to borrow against your 401(k), but use caution. Loans that are not repaid can seriously affect what is available to you at retirement. When you borrow against your 401(k) plan, you normally cannot make contributions to the program as the terms of the plan normally prohibit additional contributions until you repay the loan balance. This is a double whammy: (a) the money you borrowed is not getting tax-deferred growth, and (b) the future contributions that you cannot make will not grow tax-deferred. Even worse, if you cannot repay the loan, it will be treated as a withdrawal and will be subject to both current income taxes and a 10% early withdrawal penalty. People often get hit with this when they have an outstanding loan and want to quit their job (or get fired). Leaving the job can trigger the requirement to repay the loan immediately, which means the worker might have to register the money as an early withdrawal and then pay taxes and penalties. Instead of borrowing against your retirement, you are better off establishing an emergency fund.

How to Create an Efficient Portfolio

Diversification may be the best way to avoid losing money. Diversification, or asset allocation, is the act of dividing resources among different investment vehicles such as stocks, bonds, mutual funds, real estate, cash, etc. Doing so can lower your risk while possibly bringing an even higher return.

Why diversify?

Not all classes of assets move up and down at the same time. When stocks rise, bonds may fall. And when stocks fall, real estate may gain strength. Good asset allocation maximizes returns while guarding against disaster.

Flexibility is important

Once you have the right diversification model for meeting your goals, put your investing on autopilot. Make regular deposits, and conduct periodic reviews. It's inevitable that your asset allocation will shift with time, so rebalance your portfolio on a regular basis.

Are mutual funds diversified?

Mutual funds are often considered ready-made diversification portfolios. For example, in a balanced fund, a manager may concentrate on growth stocks and allocate lesser amounts to bonds and cash. However, a fund manager may change the fund's allocation in order to try boosting the fund's returns – thus taking on greater risk. While this may increase your portfolio's bottom line, the altered diversification model may be hurting your portfolio's long-term stability. Therefore, if you choose to diversify with mutual funds, keep a sharp eye out for shifting asset allocations that may no longer correspond with your personal requirements.

Balancing risk and reward

Efficient portfolios contain the least amount of risk for a given return. Historical analysis of diversified portfolios shows that there is an optimal mix of assets that can produce the highest return with minimal relative risk.

For example, high fuel prices are good for oil companies, but bad for airline companies who need to buy the fuel. So when oil prices rise, the stock prices of companies in these two industries can be expected to move in opposite directions. Analysts consider these two industries to have a negative (or low) correlation. Your portfolio is better diversified if you own one fuel company and one airline, rather than two oil companies.

Rather than looking at risk on an individual security level, measure the risk of an entire portfolio. When considering a security for your account, don't base your decision on the level of risk of any one investment. Rather, look at how it contributes to the overall risk of your portfolio.

Many times one particular asset class or investment does significantly well or poorly and upsets the ideal diversification model of your portfolio. Therefore, in order to bring the portfolio back into balance with the original model, assets may need to be sold and reinvested differently. Imagine your investments like your garden. Sometimes one section overgrows another and must be trimmed back. Likewise, certain areas may require extra care or water.

The Key to Asset Allocation: Determine Your Goal

Savings are important, but the most important determination of whether your savings will be sufficient may be how they are invested and what the asset allocation of your portfolio will be.

The second important rule is choosing the investments that satisfy your goal and sticking with them. Too many investors jump from company to company or one investment vehicle to another merely because of a peer recommendation. While the advice of friends and family may be well-meaning, the best asset allocation remains specific to meeting your goals, taking into consideration your individual risk tolerance and situation, current savings, and anticipated stream of income and goals.

Identify your goal

What do you want to achieve through your investments? Your goal should not be to 'make a lot of money,' but should be specific and based on your objectives and lifestyle. The 'magic number' depends on where you are in your retirement plans. Is it early in your retirement planning so you can look to long-term capital growth, or are you in need of passive income from interest, dividends, and rent on which to live?

If your goal is income, then the investment vehicles should be chosen on the basis of their income-producing capacity and lower levels of risk. A stock with a long history of consistent dividends might be a good choice even though it fluctuates in price from month to month. On the other hand, if your goal is long-term capital gains, then buying a stock with good income potential but a poor growth history might not make sense for you.

Don't over-diversify

Acquire only as many investments as you can comfortably monitor and control. ETFs and mutual funds are good diversification tools, which leave the details in the professionals' hands. One risk of over-diversification is finding the ideal investment opportunity that meets your investment goal criteria and is performing well, but the amount you have available to invest is limited because you hold too many other investments.

Find the right mix and leave it alone

A fluctuating stock price should not, by itself, motivate you to sell. Taking profits or trying to minimize short-term losses is as much of a strategy as lemmings stepping over a cliff is a planned march. Be patient with your investments. Find the right mix and leave it alone on a day-to-day basis, re-evaluating it periodically.

ADDING GLOBAL ASSETS TO YOUR RETIREMENT PORTFOLIO

Putting a portion of your retirement portfolio in another country is a good way to diversify risk on a global level. The risks associated with the economy of any single country can be mitigated by purchasing assets in other countries. Geographic diversification can be achieved through a U.S. brokerage firm by buying foreign stocks, REITs, and foreign corporate and/governmental bonds.

Examples of global investment opportunities

- Ownership of Foreign Stocks: Most major stockbrokers can purchase foreign shares on your behalf, taking care of any currency conversions if necessary. Frequently, though, and even easier, they will buy "ADRs" (American Depository Receipts), which trade like stocks on the U.S. exchanges but represent shares of foreign corporations.

- Exchange-Traded Index Funds: These are funds that track stock indices fairly closely. For example, the "MSCI EAFE" is the most well-known index for foreign investments. The acronym stands for Morgan Stanley Capital International Europe,

Australasia and Far East, and it follows the equity market performance of developed markets outside of the U.S. & Canada. There are many ETFs that track a variety of different markets and sectors.

- International Mutual Funds: There are many funds that invest in non-U.S. stocks and provide professional management overseeing the international assets.

- Foreign Asset Purchases: Acquiring assets such as real estate in countries other than your own can be done, but it usually requires more investment capital than buying stock or mutual funds. Apartment buildings, offices, and businesses can be purchased as investments, but they involve a considerable commitment of time and effort to manage them properly. Many people will buy international REITs (real estate investment trusts), which make it easier to own properties overseas since they frequently trade on the stock market.

Why bother with foreign investment opportunities?

Investing some of your retirement portfolio in international assets can hedge your portfolio against inflationary swings in the domestic economy. However, added risks include currency and political uncertainties that can devastate an account quickly.

PREPARING EMOTIONALLY FOR RETIREMENT

Retirement planning involves more than just finances. The average person spends decades getting up in the morning to go to work. Life revolves around work and careers, and, as much as you might look forward to the day when the alarm doesn't ring in the morning, being ready for that moment takes planning and preparation, emotionally, as well as financially.

Retirement brings changes

Before beginning retirement, spend time preparing for changes in all aspects of your life, not just working hours:

- *Change in who you are.* Most people identify themselves and others by what they do for a living. "David's a banker," or "Debbie works in insurance." Compare this to when someone says, "John's retired." Usually, the conversation goes on without further comment on John's activities in retirement. For better or worse, after decades in the business world people define themselves by the jobs they do rather than who they are as individuals.

- *Friendships change.* Work has a great impact on the social interactions you experience on any given day. Friendships you had at work with colleagues/clients might end unless you make a concerted effort to continue these relationships outside of the workplace. Retirees complain of the difficulty of maintaining connections from their working days because the common bond – the job – no longer exists.

- *Change in family relationships.* Spouses who spent a few hours a day together when they both worked full-time suddenly find themselves with additional time together. Conflicts on how to spend the newly-acquired time together could give rise to differences over the use of the computer, the car, or the TV. As one woman once quipped about her husband when he retired, "I married him for better or for worse, but not for lunch!"

Planning for retirement changes

Instead of "retiring from work," consider "retiring to" a hobby or goal. Instead of considering retirement as the day you stop going to work, make it the day you start [fill in the blank with your personal goal]. Prepare a retirement activity plan while you are still employed.

Being retired does not mean that you have to give up the skills and knowledge you acquired while working. Keep those skills active by volunteering, consulting, or taking classes. If nothing else, staying current will give you something to talk about with your friends from work who have not retired. Discuss with family members your post-retirement plans. Identify potential areas of conflict and work out a plan to avoid them.

Preparing for Retirement in Your 20s

If retirement planning is a marathon, then getting off to a good start and pacing yourself are the keys to victory. Setting the pace in your 20s, building on it through your 30s and 40s, and then picking up the pace as you enter your 50s is better than getting off to a late start and trying to sprint your way to the finish line.

For many folks, their 20s represent a period of transition as they move away from the limited responsibilities of adolescence toward assuming a greater role in their own well-being. If you are in your 20s, retirement is probably the furthest thing from your mind. Establishing yourself in a career, paying off school loans, and living expenses outweigh concerns about how you will be spending your retirement years, but starting now can reap huge financial rewards later.

Develop good financial habits

Develop the habit of living below your means. Don't spend your entire salary every month. A simple thing like brown-bagging it at work can add up if you invest what you would normally be spending on lunches. Use a lunch savings calculator to see how a small change in your lifestyle can have a significant impact on your retirement fund.

Create a budget and use it to monitor your spending and savings. As your family grows, your budget will too. But having a budget and learning to live within its constraints will serve you well in the future.

Don't ignore your boss

Make sure you participate fully in any work-sponsored pension plans, adding the most pre-tax dollars that you can. And don't stop there. Begin a personal savings program, no matter how small, to get into the habit of investing.

Avoid debt

If you avoid debt from an early age, you will never have to learn to manage it, since you won't have any! Credit cards offer a convenient way to make purchases, but high-interest credit card debt can quickly become overwhelming. Live the lifestyle you can afford with the money you earn by limiting your credit card purchases to what you can afford to pay in full when the monthly statement arrives. Debt and its interest payments are expensive. They should be the first line item to be cut from your budget.

Preparing for Retirement in Your 30s

The 30s represent an expansion of responsibilities, as family, home, and career take center stage. Don't ignore long-term savings and retirement planning in favor of more immediate needs. Even though your kids may need new shoes, continue building your savings.

Maximize or begin your retirement contributions

Now is the time to take maximum advantage of the tax savings and matching contributions associated with your employer-sponsored retirement plan. Review your contributions and take full advantage of the plan by increasing those contributions to the maximum amount that you can afford.

In addition to work-sponsored retirement plans, make sure you regularly contribute to your personal savings plans. First, confirm that your emergency fund is as large as it needs to be. Then, make sure you put some money aside for retirement. And then, don't forget to put aside for the non-emergency fund, college tuition fund, wedding fund, etc. Pay into your savings before engaging in discretionary spending.

Investing for growth

At this point, your investments should be growth (not income) orientated. Time is on your side to weather the inevitable turbulence of the market. It may be appropriate to add high-quality growth corporations and diversify with global and domestic funds. While it may be appropriate for someone in your stage of life to have aggressive risk profile, make sure you don't take on more risk than you are comfortable with, and that you do your due diligence on investments with professional guidance.

Teach good habits to your children

Teaching smart financial habits to your children can benefit you in two ways. Firstly, if you teach them well, they will become financially independent adults. And secondly, since they will be financially smart, they may not ask you for monetary gifts/loans that you cannot afford to give. They will grow up knowing that their wedding party has to fit within the budget of your financial plan and not keep up with the latest wedding fashions. Teaching these habits when your children are young will give them time to internalize the lessons, possibly avoiding friction when they are older.

Preparing for Retirement in Your 40s

By the time you reach your 40s, your career and earning capacity are growing. Unfortunately, short-term financial needs and responsibilities might conflict with your long-term retirement plans. Furthermore, you might begin to take care of elderly parents in addition to your children. Added caretaking responsibilities may mean less time for work, and added expenses.

Look at where you are and where you want to be

Review (or create!) your retirement plan with your financial advisor. Now is a good time to discuss changes in your current lifestyle and tweak your budget to pay for those changes.

Review your investment strategy and asset allocation to determine if they match your long-term goals. This is also a good time to review your life insurance and long-term disability insurance to make sure they provide adequate coverage to meet your family's needs.

Examine your emergency fund

Your financial responsibilities grew along with your family, and so should your emergency fund. One of the best ways to avoid depleting retirement savings to pay emergency costs and expenses is by having a fund designated just for emergencies. Make sure your emergency fund is large enough to cover three to nine months' worth of non-discretionary expenses.

Maximize contributions to your 401(k), IRA, and other tax-deferred pension plans

Adjust your contributions to your retirement plans to stay on target to meet your long-range retirement goals. Try to contribute the maximum allowable by law for the particular retirement plan.

You should also continue adding bonuses, tax-refunds, and other such one-off lump sums you receive to your retirement savings. An easy way to do this is to ask the IRS to deposit your federal income tax refund directly into your savings, as opposed to your checking account. Just check a box on your tax return and provide the account information. If you are now living in Israel, ask your tax advisor about the status of your Roth IRA or 401(k), contributions, and payouts according to Israeli tax law.

Preparing for Retirement in Your 50s

In your 50s, some of life's pressures may be easing as your children begin setting up families of their own. You should review your will and make sure it still reflects your wishes, especially since your assets are probably nearing their peak.

Catch-up time has arrived

The government wants to help you meet your retirement goals. The Internal Revenue Code allows the 50+ crowd to make increased contributions to their IRA or 401(k). Take advantage of this opportunity and increase your contributions. These "catch-up" contributions can make a big difference in reaching your retirement goals if demands on your finances made it impossible for you to maximize your contributions in the past.

If you are contributing the allowable maximums into your 401(k) and IRA retirement accounts, talk to your financial advisor about increasing contributions to taxable accounts, and possibly rebalancing your portfolio to focus more on maintaining purchasing power rather than increased growth.

Avoiding temptation

A child's wedding, purchase of a second property, or other significant events in your life might offer the temptation to withdraw from your retirement fund. Early withdrawals from retirement accounts are taxable and subject to penalties. Unless you replace the money, withdrawals can quickly reduce the size of your retirement fund.

The better alternative is planning for milestone events or major purchases well in advance by starting a savings fund earmarked specifically for them. By the time you reach your 50s, planning and saving should be familiar parts of your life.

Set a target date

You should know by now whether retirement is five, 10, or 15 years away. This information will allow you and your advisor to make appropriate adjustments in your retirement savings plan and allocation strategy.

The meeting with your financial advisor will include a review of the income stream your investments will generate during your retirement years. Look upon it as a retirement paycheck. Review your asset allocation model to make sure that it not only includes growth and income, but also preservation of principal.

AVOID COMMON MISTAKES OF RETIREMENT PLANNING

Investing is complex, but needn't be complicated. Before making any investment, do your homework, and research how you will invest your hard-earned money. While investments should be personalized for your unique situation, there are several traps that should be avoided:

If it's too good to be true, it is

Bernie Madoff was the former chair of NASDAQ and a respected member of the financial community when the bubble burst on his $64.8 billion Ponzi scheme in 2008. Among Madoff's 4,800 clients were astute business executives and financially savvy people who were tempted by the promise of a return on investment that exceeded all other investment opportunities. As the world now knows, it was all too good to be true.

If you find an unusual investment opportunity that promises higher than normal returns, investigate thoroughly. If you still think it's a worthwhile opportunity, begin with a small investment. Monitor your investment before risking a significant amount of your savings on what could become the next Ponzi scheme.

The "next sure thing"

Someone always seems to have "a tip from a friend who works in the company" about the next sure thing to hit the stock market. First, investing based on insider information is illegal. Secondly, the stock usually plummets. Talk to your financial planner before jumping head first into the "next sure thing" with your retirement fund.

Sitting at home on your computer does not make you an investment guru

Stories abound about people who day-traded on their home computers and made a fortune. However, though anecdotes may abound on the internet, for the vast majority of the participants, the losses usually significantly outweigh the gains. The real stories are about the day traders who lose their fortune with poorly timed and poorly researched trades. The SEC describes it well on their website: "While day trading is neither illegal nor is it unethical, it can be highly risky. Most individual investors do not have the wealth, the time, or the temperament to make money and to sustain the devastating losses that day trading can bring."

Real estate always goes up in value?

Even though there is a limited amount of land, scarcity doesn't always make real estate values increase. Remember the burst American housing bubble in 2008 that then spread around the world? Real estate values rose for more than a decade, and then the market collapsed. As with other assets, real estate values normally fluctuate. It can be a good investment, but only for a portion of your retirement fund. Real estate is a non-liquid asset that you must commit to as a long-term investment.

THE RETIREMENT BUDGET

During your working years and "accumulation stage," your salary helped define the size of your budget. But now, in retirement, with pensions replacing portions of your paycheck and the difference needed to be taken out of savings, your budget may need to be revised.

Meeting basic needs

Focus your attention on meeting the non-discretionary necessities of life. Food, clothing, housing, transportation, and health care are just some of the essentials of life that must be part of retirement budget. Be realistic in setting up this portion of your budget. Remember that healthcare costs will usually increase as you get older, and housing expenses grow due to property taxes and home repair costs. Depending on location and other factors, downsizing your house may not necessary translate into "less expensive."

Discretionary expenses

Discretionary expenses are the costs of the things you want, but if need be, can live without. Travel, entertainment, and hobbies might be important elements of your retirement lifestyle, but they are not life essentials. You can scale back on your travel plans more easily than you can cut back on food or shelter. Discretionary expenses are in the "I want" portion of your budget instead of the "I need" section.

How much do you need?

Estimates vary, but 70 to 80 percent of your pre-retirement annual earnings should meet the lifestyle needs of most people in retirement. Granted, a more lavish lifestyle will increase the percentages, while a more frugal lifestyle will decrease them.

For guidance about where your lifestyle choice puts you as far as budgetary needs, go through the following list and mark each with a plus if you expect to pay more in retirement or a minus if you expect to spend less:

- Mortgage or rent

- Debt repayment

- Travel

- Large-scale purchases, such as for new furniture or a new car

- Medical care and medical insurance

- Taxes

If more of the items on the list have plus marks than minuses, then your retirement budget should be equal to or more than your annual earnings while you were working. This might also be a good time to sit down with your financial planner to review your anticipated retirement lifestyle so that it does not conflict with your retirement savings plan. If it does, then you must either make changes to your retirement lifestyle plans or increase your contributions to the retirement fund in order to meet your budgeted expenses.

Why You Should *Not* Count on Pensions or Social Security

Fears of U.S. Social Security benefits not being available to the young workers of today when they reach retirement age are probably unfounded... *probably*. Of course, that does not mean that today's workers can expect to have the same benefits or retirement age at which they can begin collecting as workers reaching retirement age in 2013. And in Israel, the basic state pension is currently fairly low (at around ₪1,500 in 2013), and we don't know what this figure will be in the future.

Public and private pension plans are not as stable as they used to be. In the United States, more than 1,400 companies discontinued their pension plans in 2011.[1] This is a 14.3% increase in discontinued pension plans from 2009. Instead of looking at pension plans as *the* source of retirement income, perhaps it is time to look at pension plans (both governmental and employer) as a *supplement* to personal savings.

---

1   According to the Pension Benefit Guaranty Corp.

What to expect from American Social Security

President Obama's deficit reduction panel addressed the future of Social Security and recommended the following:

- *Increases in the retirement age.* The full retirement age for Social Security is currently 66 for those born in 1943 through 1954 and increases two months a year for those born in 1955 and later until it reaches an age 67 maximum. Proposals for change would allow the retirement age to continue to rise. When social security began, lifespans were shorter, and payments were received for fewer years. It may not be possible for governments (under current taxation levels) to subsidize many decades of retirement income as lifespans continue to increase.

- *High earners get lower benefits.* Those who earn $106,800 a year during their working years would receive 30% reduction in benefits under the deficit panel's proposals.

- *Reductions in cost of living increases.* Cuts in Social Security cost of living increases were proposed and, if approved, would make a substantial impact on the total amount of income received by longer living retirees, who may no longer be able to make a set income meet inflation-swelled bills.

Planning and saving

Whether your retirement income is from Social Security or a pension plan, the way to protect yourself from changes in your pension plan or Social Security is to talk to your financial planner about the strategies you can implement in your personal savings plan. Together with your advisor, map out a savings strategy designed for saving towards your future retirement.

Applying for Social Security

Should you opt-in to receive Social Security benefits at 62 years of age or wait until your full retirement age? If you plan to continue working, the answer could be "no."

In 2013, if you earn more than $15,120, your monthly benefits will be reduced by $1 for every $2 earned over the limit. However, the limit doesn't apply to money earned before you begin collecting Social Security benefits, and there are no restrictions on what you can earn after you reach your full retirement age.

In Israel, the situation is fairly similar. Men may receive a government pension from age 67 and for women from 62. But this is also affected by your level of income. For example, if you earn between ₪5,032 - ₪7,285, you may be able to claim only a partial pension. If you earn more than ₪7,285, you may not be entitled to a pension at all. This situation continues until the age of 70 for men and 65 for women, when you can claim an old age pension irrespective of income.

What are earnings?

Unemployment payments and pension or retirement withdrawals do not count as earnings for Social Security purposes. Also excluded from earnings is investment income. The limitations only apply to the money you earn from working.

In Israel, if you receive income from sources other than work of up to ₪15,096 (in 2013) if you're single, and up to ₪20,127 if you're married, you may receive the full amount of *Bituach Leumi.*

How to apply for early or full retirement benefits

To apply for benefits from Social Security, go to the Social Security website three months before you want your monthly payments to begin. You need to provide the following information:

- Date and place of birth
- Social Security number
- Name, Social Security number, and date of birth of your current spouse and any former spouses
- Names of unmarried children under 18, or between 18 and 19 and in secondary school
- Routing number and account number of your bank account for direct deposit
- Citizenship status
- The month benefits are to begin

You must report any work performed outside the United States if it exceeds 45 hours a month. All applicants must furnish a W-2 for the work year prior to applying for Social Security. Self-employed individuals must furnish a copy of their tax return. If you do not have any of the documents requested during the application process, you should submit the application with the information you have. You can submit other documents later.

If you want to apply for an old age pension in Israel, you must go to the nearest branch of *Bituach Leumi* (National Insurance Institute) and fill out an old age pension claim form.

Taxes on your Social Security benefits

Social Security benefits are taxable. Up to 85 percent of your benefits are subject to taxes if a married couple's combined income exceeds $44,000 a year. If a couple's combined income is between $32,000 and $44,000, then 50 percent of their income might be taxable. However, there is some good news here. Because of a tax treaty between the United States and Israel, if you live in Israel and collect American Social Security, you do not have to pay tax on that income in either jurisdiction... and vice versa. Make sure you review your own situation with a qualified accountant to make sure you get all of the details correct.

Social Security
Spousal Benefit

Spouses and widows/widowers are entitled to Social Security benefits based on their own record of earnings or that of their spouse. This is true even if you never worked and paid into the Social Security system. You are eligible as long as you are at least 62 years of age and your spouse receives or is eligible to receive retirement benefits. In Israel, there is a "spousal increment" that is added to the old age pension.

Monthly benefit amount

If you have not reached full retirement age, but you qualify for benefits based on your own record of contributions, Social Security pays you the amount to which your work record/contributions entitles you. If you qualify for a higher monthly payment as a spouse, Social Security pays you the higher amount.

When you reach full retirement age, you are entitled to receive up to one half of your spouse's monthly full retirement benefit. The payments you receive as a spouse do not affect the payments that your spouse gets. Money you receive from a pension from another government pension or from a foreign employer could reduce the amount of Social Security you get.

Retirement planning options using the spousal benefit

If your spouse has reached full retirement age, your spouse can apply for benefits, but request that they be suspended. This allows you to obtain spousal benefits while your spouse earns delayed retirement credits that increase monthly benefits until age 70.

If you are at full retirement age, you can elect to take spousal benefits and delay taking benefits based on your own record of contributions. You could qualify later for delayed retirement credits by doing this.

Widows and widowers

A widow or widower might be entitled to benefits at age 60, or if the person is disabled, at age 50, based on the earnings of the deceased spouse. Remarriage after 60 years of age does not affect the widow/widower's eligibility to receive benefits.

Benefits are available to a widow or widower who cares for the couple's child who is under 16 or is disabled. In this situation, a widow/widower who hasn't remarried may receive benefits at any age.

SOCIAL SECURITY AND DIVORCE

When one spouse works outside the home and the other remains at home, the stay-at-home spouse might not be eligible for Social Security benefits, apart from spousal benefits. However, in the event of divorce, Social Security recognizes the stay-at-home spouse's contributions to the marriage by extending spousal benefits, but with some limitations.

Eligibility for benefits after a divorce

If your marriage lasted for at least 10 years, you might be eligible for Social Security retirement benefits based on your ex-spouse's earnings record, as long as you have not remarried and you are 62 years of age or older. Remarriage after age 60 will not disqualify you from benefits if your ex-spouse is deceased.

You cannot collect benefits in this manner if you are entitled to them on your own, and your benefits are greater than what you would receive through your ex-spouse. Your receipt of benefits won't affect anything that your ex-spouse will receive.

When can you apply?

You can apply at the age of 62, or 60 if your ex-spouse is deceased, as long as your ex-spouse would be entitled to benefits. You can receive benefits even if your ex-spouse has not applied, provided your divorce was at least two years ago and your ex-spouse is at least 62 years of age when you apply.

If your ex-spouse has not reached 62 years of age, but you have, you can apply under your earnings record. Once your ex-spouse reaches 62, you can switch to the higher benefit under your ex-spouse's record of earnings.

Amount and duration of benefit

A divorced spouse claiming benefits on an ex-spouse's account can receive up to 50 percent of the amount the ex-spouse would receive at full retirement age. Benefits cease if the spouse claiming benefits remarries and the ex-spouse is alive.

Delayed retirement credits

You might be eligible for benefits under your own account and also as an ex-spouse. In that case, you can collect as an ex-spouse and delay taking your own benefits. This strategy may give you the advantage of a higher monthly benefit when you reach the age of 70.

In Israel, the laws in this case are somewhat different. For example, a stay-at-home wife in Israel is entitled to an old age pension if she paid monthly contributions to *Bituach Leumi*, but as a divorcee is not entitled to a spousal increment.

Discuss the options available to you as an ex-spouse with your financial planner to determine the most advantageous use of the ex-spousal benefit.

THE MYTH OF
BITUACH LEUMI

Bituach Leumi (Israel's National Insurance) is responsible for various welfare benefits, including the old age pensions of those who paid into the system. Almost everyone in Israel is expected to pay into *Bituach Leumi*. Your employer is responsible for making payments on your behalf, and self-employed workers are responsible for making their own payments. If you do not work (unemployment lasting longer than a prescribed period) or are a housewife, check with the authorities about what your specific obligations are.

How much will you get when the time comes?

Eligibility to receive the government pension depends on your gender and date of birth. Israel recently grandfathered in an older retirement age, where the retirement age men are eligible for full pension benefits is 67 and women at 62. This reflects the growing realization that the government's budget cannot continue to support a growing populations with longer lifespans.

At full retirement age, pensions are approximately NIS 1,500/month for an individual and about NIS 2,250 (total) for a couple. A couple's payment is based on an individual plus an increment for the spouse. After age

80, there is a slight increase in payment. Additional incremental increases in payments are based upon the age when you first began to receive benefits (if you postpone receiving benefits until age 70 for men and for women between 65-70, depending on date of birth) and if you paid into the system for more than ten years prior to retirement.

What if you retire early?

Bituach Leumi recognizes the fact that some people might want to retire early and work during their retirement. In both of these scenarios, retiring early and working during retirement, there are limits regarding the amount of income (both from salary and rental income) allowed if you wish to receive government benefits before reaching full retirement age. So if you wanted to retire early and work part-time, consider whether your salary will disqualify you from receiving benefits.

The solution

Don't invest in the myth of *Bituach Leumi* and believe that the government's pension will cover all your needs during retirement. *Bituach Leumi* payments, even with the incremental increases, are barely at subsistence level. Therefore, this government pension should not be considered your sole source of income in retirement, but should be looked at as a supplement to your personal savings/work pension plan payments. Let your state pension be the icing on the cake rather than the cake itself.

WORKING DURING RETIREMENT

There are several reasons why people work past traditional retirement age. Whether it is money, self-fulfillment, habit, or the need to keep on contributing to the community, more and more people choose to work part-time or full-time in their golden years.

Maybe it is all about the money

More companies and businesses are opening their doors to retirees who want to stay active and earn extra money from a part-time job. In return, the business gains a mature, reliable worker with years of experience relative to the position.

A part-time job offers the retiree an income to supplement Social Security, pension benefits, and personal savings. Some people use the income from their retirement jobs to indulge in luxuries without taking away from their retirement savings. But be careful you don't earn too much, lest your government pension get cut. Speak to your accountant to find out the specifics in your case.

Also, the longer income is coming in, the longer you can delay withdrawing money from your savings accounts. This means more time for compound interest to let your nest egg continue to grow.

Some people love their jobs

An attorney who retired after practicing law for 40 years stepped from the courtroom into the classroom, where he teaches paralegal studies at a local college. He explained that he had wanted to teach for a long time, but his work schedule never gave him the opportunity to do so. Once he retired, he was able to do something he truly loved. Have you been itching for a second career but couldn't afford to take time away from your first one? Retirement might be the perfect opportunity.

Maintaining human contact

For some people, most of their social interaction takes place at work. For them, maintaining that interaction is important, so a part-time job offers them the opportunity to enjoy having contact with people and perhaps stay in touch with former colleagues in the same industry or profession.

PROTECT YOUR
RETIREMENT FROM
INFLATION

As you read this, inflation is eating away at the value of your money. Over time, American's inflation rate has slowly eroded the value of the dollar to the point where $1 today would only have been worth 4.8 cents in 1913 dollars. Other countries and currencies aren't immune from the devastating effects of inflation either. Even though Israel's current inflation rate is a manageable 1.3 % (as of March 2013), levels since 2000 have (apart from a brief period in 2002) hovered between around 2% to 4%, according to figures published by the Ministry of Finance.

Deflation

The opposite of inflation is deflation. The Great Depression in 1929 is an example of deflation. As asset values fall, people hoard cash in order to maintain liquidity and be able to take advantage of the bargain assets for sale. The challenge in a deflationary period is that the holders of the cash continue to hold out for even lower asset values. This, in turn, slows an already slow economy even more. Declining profits, layoffs, and plummeting prices continue until the economy is caught in a cycle from which it is difficult to escape.

The solution

One hedge against inflationary or deflationary conditions affecting your retirement portfolio is to avoid having all your investments tied to one country's economy (remember geographic diversification). Instead of a portfolio composed of solely of American or Israeli stocks, bonds, Treasury bills, and real estate, include global assets as part of your retirement asset allocation.

Some people recommend other diversification possibilities, such as shifting some of your retirement investments into gold, oil, natural gas, and other investments with an intrinsic value. However, these investments carry their own risks and have disappointed many investors, so make sure to check with a professional financial advisor to see if they are appropriate for you.

Another solution to inflation is keeping a portion of your investments, even during the more conservative retirement period, in growth investments. Their growth, even if slow, can serve to counteract the debilitating force of inflation.

INCREASING INVESTMENT INCOME

What's the difference between a stock and a bond? Shares of stock represent an ownership or equity interest in a corporation, whereas a corporate bond represents a debt owed by the company to the purchaser of the bond. A bond investor normally purchases the bond he wants to collect periodic interest payments from the corporation (usually paid every six months).

Yield and risk

Generally speaking, the higher the yield on a bond, the greater the risk will be. Solid companies in good industries who have strong earnings and large cash reserves can offer lower yields to investors because the risk of default is lower. Weaker companies with high debt loads and high-risk businesses have to offer higher yields to encourage investors to purchase their bonds.

Short-term or long-term corporate bonds

Yields tend to be lower on short-term bonds because the risk of default is lower than in the case of a long-term bond. Also, people feel more certain about how the economy will look in the near term than in the long term, and because of that sense of security, companies need not pay such a high interest rate. On the other hand, if you gave a loan and would only get repaid in 30 years, since no one knows what the world will look like then, you want to receive a higher return for taking on the risk. Corporate bonds can offer investors a rate of return on their investment that is relatively high compared to bank deposits, but they also have more risk.

Investing in corporate bonds

Investors can purchase individual corporate bonds through a broker. The challenge of investing in bonds in this manner is that an investor must diversify the bonds to include different types of companies in a mix of industries and maturity dates. This can be difficult for the novice investor or an investor who does not have the time to spend researching companies and industries.

Exchange-traded funds (ETFs) and mutual funds offer diversification, and in the case of mutual funds, investors also benefit from the professional investment skills of a fund manager. Some mutual funds and ETFs offer investors the opportunity to invest in bonds issued by international companies. Some of the international funds offer investors high yields by including corporate bonds from emerging markets as well as developed markets. The benefit of global diversification can cut both ways, though. Having foreign exposure can contribute to your returns and also expose you to currency, country, political risk, and more.

Corporate bonds offer another investment vehicle for your retirement portfolio, but avoid taking on too much risk. You should not invest in a bond just because it offers the highest yield. High returns usually mean high risk. Research the company thoroughly before investing your money.

GET INCOME AT
SPECIFIC INTERVALS
DURING RETIREMENT

Imagine having $50,000 to invest in corporate bonds. You decide to purchase one bond yielding 2.5% annual interest and maturing in five years. Even if your money is tied up for five years, you might not care because you like the 2.5% interest rate. But if interest rates in the marketplace increase to 3.5 % in six months, you might not be as happy that you are "losing" 1% annually. In other words, you locked in the 2.5% rate for five years. Had you waited to buy the bonds, though, you could have gotten 3.5%.

What would happen if, instead of purchasing one bond for $50,000, you bought five bonds for $10,000 each, with maturity dates one year apart starting in one year? If interest rates increase, you can take the $10,000 from the maturing bond at the end of the first year and invest it in a new bond at the higher interest rate. On the other hand, if interest rates fall, you will only have $10,000 next year to invest into a new bond at the lower rate instead of all $50,000. This technique is called "bond laddering."

Purpose of bond laddering

Bond laddering allows you to minimize your exposure to fluctuations in interest rates while maintaining liquidity, by not committing all your money for a set term. Bond laddering allows you to diversify your bond portfolio by maturity dates. The more maturity dates you have, the more "time-diversified" your portfolio will be.

How you space the time between maturity dates will have an effect on your average return. Longer time periods between maturity dates usually means a higher average return, but you tie up your money for longer. Shorter times between the maturity dates give you access to the money, but offers a lower yield. Nevertheless, the flexibility in creating the ladders to give you payments precisely when you need them is a tool that is very attractive to retirees.

Call features on bonds

One thing to watch out for when picking bonds is a "call feature." A callable bond allows the company to redeem it earlier than the maturity date. A call feature could limit the effectiveness of your bond ladder if some of the issues you own get called earlier than you had planned.

Bond ladders offer an investor the opportunity to diversify and somewhat minimize harm from fluctuating interest rates. Consult your financial advisor to find out how bonds and a bond ladder could work in your investment portfolio.

BEWARE OF LOSING MONEY IN BONDS

While bonds are traditionally considered a safer, more conservative investment than stocks, it is possible to lose money in bonds. Yes, you read that correctly. In order to protect your principal while investing in bonds, be wary of the following:

Interest rate fluctuations

Bond prices decline when interest rates rise. If you incorrectly predict the direction in which interest rates are heading, you could lose money with your bonds. However, if you hold the bonds to maturity and the issuers don't default, then you will get back the full face value of the bond regardless of interest rates in the marketplace.

Credit rating agencies

Companies and governments are both susceptible to downward ratings of creditworthiness by credit rating agencies. A bad quarter of earnings or a reported event might trigger action by the credit rating agencies. Investors can lose money on a decline in the bond issuer's credit rating.

Inflation

You will lose money if the earnings in your bond portfolio don't outpace inflation. When inflation is running high, consider using U.S. Treasury inflation-protected securities or inflation-linked corporate and municipal bonds. Even though these inflation-linked securities offer lower interest rates than non-linked issues, their linkage to inflation could protect your purchasing power.

Restructuring

Mergers, acquisitions, and capital restructuring are standard occurrences in the business world. Corporate bonds can drop in value when a major change occurs in the company. Reviewing the reasons for the changes in the corporation and the overall financial shape of the company might not avoid the problem, but it might help you determine whether to hold the bond or sell it.

Exchange controls

If you own bonds issued in a country other than your own and do not know what exchange controls are, take a seat. Exchange controls are how the country in which the bonds were issued imposes a ban on the removal of money from its borders. In some cases, governments might restrict the flow of capital out of their borders (as Cyprus had to do to protect its banking industry in 2013). If that happens at a time when you expect to receive an interest or principal payment from a bond issued in that country, you might be stuck holding a worthless security.

Foreign currency exchange rate fluctuations

When there are unfavorable currency exchange rates between the country in which you live and the country where the bond was issued, you may lose money.

Foreign nationalization

You want to achieve global asset allocation for your retirement portfolio, so you decide to invest in bonds in a country with which you are completely unfamiliar. After purchasing the bonds, you discover that the government of the tropical paradise in which the issuing corporation is located just nationalized all of the businesses in the country. The government now owns the issuer of your bond and may simply choose to default on the loan.

Liquidity

Just because you want to sell a bond you own, you may not be able to find a buyer. Bonds tend to be less liquid than stocks, which means that if you need the money right away, you may have to sell the bond for a much lower price than you would have expected, or you may possibly not be able to sell it at all.

Municipal bonds may not be tax free

Municipal bonds are much more complicated than they appear. One big risk that often surprises investors is when they discover that these tax-free bonds aren't actually tax free at all. A common case of this is when people move to Israel and discover that their "munis" are taxable in Israel. The Israeli tax authority does not view these bonds as tax free, so make sure that you update your portfolio when you leave the United States.

CHOOSE A BOND FUND FOR GREATER DIVERSIFICATION

Bond funds offer investors an opportunity for diversification and professional management.

Fund performance

Just because a mutual fund company buys bonds, owners of the fund still must accept certain risks. One example is "interest rate risk," which means that as interest rates rise, bond values fall. Therefore, the money you invest in a bond fund can decrease during periods of rising interest rates in the economy. And the opposite is true, too. If you own a bond fund, and interest rates in the world drop, the bonds inside the fund will appear more attractive on the market and the value of the fund should appreciate. A fund's sensitivity to fluctuations in interest rates depends upon the duration of its holdings. Bonds with a longer duration tend to be more volatile than bonds with shorter durations.

Though time frames are not exact, investors generally consider funds as "short-term" if their holdings mature between zero to 3.5 years, "intermediate-term" if they are 3.5 to six years, and "long-term" if they are longer than six years.

Another indicator of a bond fund's performance is its credit quality. Credit quality is the creditworthiness of the company or entity issuing the bonds as determined by bond rating agencies.

High-yield funds usually involve more risk because they buy low-quality bonds (often called "junk bonds"). High credit-quality bond funds include investment holdings with high average credit values.

Knowing a fund's duration and credit quality allows you to determine the risk level of your investment.

Diversifying your bond investments

Getting the right mix of bond types is important for achieving a well-rounded investment portfolio. You can achieve this by investing in a combination of government bond funds, mortgage-backed bond funds, corporate bond funds, municipal bond funds, and global bond funds. You do not have to invest in all of these types of funds. The mix that works for you depends upon your investment goals and the amount of risk you are willing to accept.

Investing in bond funds does not require the same knowledge as is required to select individual bonds in which to invest, but evaluating bond funds is important for the success of your investments. Consult with your financial advisor before investing in bonds or bond funds.

DO DIVIDEND-PAYING STOCKS PROVIDE ENOUGH INCOME?

Stocks that pay dividends with predictable regularity might not post spectacular price gains, but they can be a reliable source of income for investors approaching retirement age.

Equity ownership

When a corporation sells shares of its own stock, these represent ownership in the company. In other words, a purchaser of even just one share of stock in a company is an owner of the company, albeit a very small owner. As a company prospers, it has the option to reinvest profits back into the business. A shareholder benefits from this investment of profits as the company grows and the value of its shares of stock increase.

Another way for a shareholder to benefit from a company's profits is to receive a portion of the profits as a direct payment from the company in the form of a payment called a *dividend*.

Entitlement to dividends

When a corporation announces a decision to pay a dividend to shareholders instead of reinvesting all profits back into the business, this is known as a *declaration date*. But not all shareholders are entitled to receive a declared dividend. Only the owners of shares issued prior to a date, known as the *ex-dividend date,* may receive the declared dividend. People who purchased their shares after the ex-dividend date can participate in future dividend declarations, but are not entitled to the current one.

Using dividends for retirement income

Some companies have a history of declaring dividends on a regular basis. For example, Coca-Cola has a long history of paying dividends to its shareholders. Its dividends have steadily increased since 1962. A stock with a history of increasing the amount of its dividends from year to year might be a good source of income. Stockholders have a choice of receiving the dividend as a quarterly payment, or in some cases, to use the dividends to purchase additional shares of stock through a dividend reinvestment plan.

Finding dividend-paying stocks

Your financial planner might be able to recommend companies with a history of paying dividends and those companies whose dividends have increased each year as a hedge against inflation. Your advisor might also recommend dividend income funds that invest in stocks with a history of paying dividends. The dividends collected by the income fund are distributed to the fund's investors. Some funds offer a dividend reinvestment plan for those individuals who do not need or want the income payment.

CHOOSING REAL ESTATE
AS AN INVESTMENT

While it's tempting to think of your house as an "investment," your primary residence shouldn't be thought of as funding your nest egg. If you feel compelled to invest in real estate, consider some of the following:

Residential real estate

Single-family homes, apartment buildings, condominiums, and cooperative apartments are the most common forms of residential real estate. You can purchase unoccupied residential property and find your own tenants, or you can purchase property with an existing tenant.

The drawback to buying a property that has existing tenants is that you are locked into a lease that was negotiated by the former owner. Review the lease with your attorney to make certain there are no surprises and the terms are acceptable to you.

Commercial real estate

Office buildings and small warehouses are the most common types of commercial real estate. Just as with residential property, be sure to review existing leases to make sure the current terms are acceptable to you.

Simply becoming the new owner of a building does not allow you to change the lease of an existing tenant.

Industrial real estate

Car washes, storage facilities, and parking garages are examples of industrial real estate, where you acquire the real estate and a business that generates revenue from sales or services to the public. This type of real estate investment requires more management than the passive income generated from rents, due to the business component that comes along with the property.

Retail real estate

Storefronts, shopping malls, strip malls, and other retail outlets are the most common types of retail real estate. An important factor to investigate before investing in retail real estate is the strength of the local economy and the likelihood that you will be able to rent out the property.

Mix-use real estate

Some properties combine commercial and retail or commercial and residential into one building. One example would be a building with retail stores on the ground floor and offices or apartments on the second floor. Mix-use properties might offer lower risk than single-use properties because of the diversification they offer in attracting tenants.

Real Estate Investment Trusts (REITs)

REITs own a diverse portfolio of real estate or mortgages. Investment in a REIT is done in much the same manner as purchasing shares of stock, and you don't have to deal with the whole processing of buying and selling, nor managing an actual property. Many people use REITs to get real estate exposure without the hassles of being a landlord.

Real Estate Investment Trusts (REITs)

REITs: Real Estate Investment Trusts

A Real Estate Investment Trust, or REIT, feels a lot like a mutual fund that owns different properties. REITs enable people to pool their money with other investors and then have professional management teams acquire and manage real-estate holdings for investment purposes. In order to maintain its special tax status, a REIT must meet the following criteria:

- It distributes 90% of its annual taxable income to shareholders as dividends.

- It invests 75% of its assets in real estate, mortgages, other REITs, cash, or government securities.

- It derives 75% of its gross income from rents, mortgage interest, or real property sales.

- It has at least 100 shareholders, with fewer than 50% of the shares in the hands of five or fewer shareholders.

Advantages of REITs

REITs offer the opportunity to invest in real estate with professional managers handling the acquisition and management of the properties. A person with $10,000 available to invest in real estate can have the benefit of a portfolio of diversified real-estate holdings by purchasing REIT shares.

REITs offer greater liquidity than traditional brick and mortar real estate ownership. Shares in a REIT can be sold on the stock market to allow an investor to move money into other investments. Compare that to selling a home or commercial property on your own, which could take months or years. As REITs provide cash dividends, they may be a good fit for a retiree looking for additional income.

Because of the tax advantages afforded to REITs, the rental income the REIT receives is not taxed, so it avoids the double taxation that occurs when a corporation pays taxes on its profits and the shareholders pay taxes when those same profits are distributed as dividends.

Types of REITs

There are three main types of REITs - equity, mortgage, and hybrid.

An equity REIT is a corporation that buys, renovates, manages, and sells real estate. Equity REITs frequently concentrate on the acquisition of a specific type or use of real estate. For example, you can find residential REITs, healthcare REITs, and retail REITs.

Mortgage REITs acquire and hold loans secured by mortgage liens on real estate. Unlike other types of

REITs, mortgage REITs invest in loans and not the actual real estate securing the debt.

Hybrid REITs combine equity and mortgage REITs. A hybrid might own a portfolio of mortgage-secured loans as one component, and it might have ownership interests in other real estate.

Well-diversified retirement portfolios often use REITs, as well as other income-producing investments, to shore up their monthly income requirements. Ask your financial advisor if you should include them in your account, too.

PREFERRED STOCK

When people talk about buying stocks, they talk about buying shares in a company. However, not all shares are identical, and different types of stock have different advantages. One type of stock that sometimes acts like a bond is called a preferred stock.

What are preferred stocks?

All public companies have common stock, but some may choose to offer preferred shares. These preferred shares have priority over common shares in bankruptcy proceedings and the distribution of dividends.

Though preferred shares often pay higher dividends than the common shares of the same company, the corporation frequently has the right to redeem preferred shares at any time. This means that the corporation can "call" them, that is, buy them back from the shareholder at a predetermined price. If you were counting on the ongoing income stream from the investment, that "call" could hurt your cash flow.

Preferred shares sometimes have the term "cumulative" in their description. In other words, if a corporation owes a preferred dividend but it cannot pay it out because of a shortage of cash, the amount owed to the preferred shareholders will accumulate until such time as the company can pay in full... and before the common shareholders can get anything.

Buying preferred stock

Common stocks and preferred stocks are listed in the same manner in financial newspapers and websites. A preferred stock is often purchased through a broker in the same way as is a common stock, though they might also be traded with a spread, and the brokerage firm and traders make money between the "bid" and "ask" prices.

Evaluating preferred stock

Like corporate bonds, rating companies such as Standard & Poor's rate preferred stocks by using letters to signify grade. The highest rating is "AAA."A "BBB-" rating and above is considered investment grade. Below "BBB-" is considered junk grade.

Preferred stocks can afford the investor a higher return on investment than bonds, though because they have fixed dividend payments and very long (or no) maturity dates, they often go down in price when interest rates go up. Consider them for your retirement portfolio if you are prepared to take on the added risk in exchange for the higher potential return.

ARE JUNK BONDS
WORTH THE HIGHER YIELD?

Higher yield usually means greater risk. Frequently, investors are mesmerized by high-yield bonds and ignore the reason for the high yield. Higher yield bonds mean that there is a greater chance the bond might default. Investing in a bond fund or an exchange-traded fund diversifies away some of the risk, but won't completely protect you from defaults on principal or interest payments.

Who issues high-yield bonds?

Small corporations that have yet to prove themselves in the marketplace or larger businesses in financial distress are the two most likely types of companies to issue high-yield bonds. Although risky, high-yield bonds can provide diversification in an investment portfolio when combined with other investment vehicles.

Benefits of high-yield bonds

During periods of economic distress, high-yield bonds have often outperformed stocks. The greater volatility of high-yield bonds over other segments of the bond market offers investors high income and potential capital appreciation over the long term. However, high-yield bonds aren't short-term investments, and anyone who is not prepared to stay with them over the long term should avoid them.

Impact of interest rates

High-yield bonds have a tendency to go against current wisdom about rising interest rates causing a decline in the bond market, and they seem to be affected less than the rest of the bond market by changes in prevailing interest rates.

Default rates

The volatility of high-yield bonds is a real concern for investors. When the market turns sour, high-yield bond values can fall rapidly. Over the past three decades, high-yield bond issuers have had a default rate of around 4.5% a year. In bad times, that rate was around 12% and in good times it was under 2%. Therefore, high-yield bonds aren't for the faint of heart or those unwilling to monitor their portfolio's performance and economic conditions on a continual basis.

After all, there is a reason high-yield bonds are referred to as "junk bonds."

Watch Out for Reverse Mortgages

Financial advisors generally suggest having all loans and debts, including mortgages, paid off before retirement. This is because it is difficult enough to meet daily expenses on a fixed income, let alone make loan payments with potentially high interest rates. As such, taking out a loan during retirement is frowned upon. But what about a reverse mortgage, which refers to borrowing against your home's equity?

What is a reverse mortgage?

A reverse mortgage is a loan that is secured by a mortgage filed against your home. If you are 62 years of age or older, a bank or other lender will allow you to borrow up to the amount of equity you have built up in your home. Unlike a home equity loan that requires repayment in monthly installments, a reverse mortgage lender pays the loan proceeds to you in monthly installments. Like other mortgage-secured loans, interest is added to the amount of the debt in a reverse mortgage, and loan fees charged by the lender can be substantial.

The payments to the borrower continue until the loan proceeds are exhausted or the borrower dies. A borrower who is still alive and living in the home when the payments end is not required to repay the debt until the home is sold or the estate pays.

Risks associated with reverse mortgages

The rules and documents associated with a reverse mortgage are complex and confusing. Have an attorney and financial advisor review the reverse mortgage terms and documentation before you sign anything.

Reverse mortgages are due on the death of the borrower. If only one spouse borrows under a reverse mortgage, the surviving spouse could be placed in the position of needing to repay the debt, possibly even selling the house to do so.

Reverse mortgages offer an alternative to home equity loans for those seniors who must access the equity in their homes, but using them as a source of income can unnecessarily place your home at risk if you don't pay the property taxes on the home or keep it insured.

CONCLUSION

Reading this book is the beginning of your journey toward achieving your retirement goals. You reached your first milestone by breaking away from the 50% of the American workforce that has not started planning for retirement.

Setting and reaching your financial goals for retirement are important milestones. The information presented in this book hopefully provided you with direction and specific action steps, but remember, retirement planning doesn't end on the day you retire.

Retirement planning is an ongoing process that requires periodic review and adjustment in order to meet the challenges life presents. Once retired, you still need to review your expenditures and your budget diligently and constantly make certain your income is keeping pace with your lifestyle's demands.

The good news is that studies show that people who calculate how much they need for retirement tend to have higher savings goals than people who don't spend time thinking about retirement. Those who have a concrete plan that they refer to on an ongoing basis are likely to meet their aims.

When planning for retirement, stay on track. Remember that your financial advisor is only a phone call away, so take advantage of that whenever questions or concerns threaten to get in the way of enjoying your retirement years.

Here's hoping that at your retirement party you'll have something to celebrate... a well-planned retirement!

Index

■■■■■■■■■■■■■■■■■■■■■■■■■■■■■■■■

www.ingramcontent.com/pod-product-compliance
Lightning Source LLC
Chambersburg PA
CBHW021425180326
41458CB00001B/134